# THE PERSONAL BAGGAGE RULE IMPORT EXPORT IN INDIA

**ASHOK KHANNA**

**BLUEROSE PUBLISHERS**
India | U.K.

Copyright © Ashok Khanna 2025

All rights reserved by author. No part of this publication may be reproduced, stored in a retrieval system or transmitted in any form or by any means, electronic, mechanical, photocopying, recording or otherwise, without the prior permission of the author. Although every precaution has been taken to verify the accuracy of the information contained herein, the publisher assumes no responsibility for any errors or omissions. No liability is assumed for damages that may result from the use of information contained within.

BlueRose Publishers takes no responsibility for any damages, losses, or liabilities that may arise from the use or misuse of the information, products, or services provided in this publication.

For permissions requests or inquiries regarding this publication, please contact:

BLUEROSE PUBLISHERS
www.BlueRoseONE.com
info@bluerosepublishers.com
+91 8882 898 898
+4407342408967

ISBN: 978-93-7018-355-1

Cover Design: Shubham Verma
Typesetting: Sagar

First Edition: April 2025

# About Ashok Khanna

Date of Birth: Born in 1954.

Professional Experience: Active in the logistics, relocation, and customs agent business since 1977.

Expertise:
Specializes in import-export processes, with a focus on:

- Baggage and personal imports.
- Customs duties for cars.
- Foreign exchange for travellers.
- Import and export of gifts and miscellaneous items.

## Contributions to the Industry

With over four decades of experience, Ashok Khanna has developed unparalleled knowledge of logistics, customs, and import-export processes. His expertise includes:

- **Rules and Regulations:**
    - A detailed understanding of India's import-export policies.
    - Practical insights into navigating customs clearance and documentation requirements.
- **Guidance:**
    - Advice on foreign exchange rules for travellers.
    - Guidance on duty assessment, especially for baggage, personal items, and vehicles.
- **Specimen Documents:**
    - Sharing detailed templates and step-by-step guides for customs documentation to help individuals avoid errors and delays.

---

# Purpose

The aim is to make Ashok Khanna's extensive knowledge and experience available to those dealing with the complexities of international logistics and customs. By sharing insights, templates, and rules, individuals can navigate the often-daunting processes with ease and confidence.

# Index of Topics and Resources and pages

1. Import-Export Policy          1
2. Baggage Rules          1
   - Accompanied baggage.    2
   - Green and Red channel    3
   - Rules under transfer of residence. 3-5
   - Delay in shipment. 4-5
3. **Annexures**
   - Annexure 1: prohibited List of items. 5-6
   - Annexure 2: List of restricted items. 5-6, 42
   - Annexure 3: permissible Duty-exempt items for personal imports by diplomats. 6
4. Customs Duty and Calculations      6-7
   - Question-Answer section on duty calculations. 7-8
   - Re-imported baggage. 8
   - Import of foodstuff by foreigners. 9
   - Customs duty on laptops, jewellery, and Indian currency export/import. 9
5. Foreign Exchange        10
   - Regulations for travellers.    10
   - Export of Indian currency    10

6. Restricted Items 11

   Unaccompanied baggage 11,30,31

   Exemptions for certain articles 32,33

   Special concession for foreign officials 33

   Transfer of residence for foreign national 34,36

   Export of food stuff for Govt. Officials 13

   Export commercial goods as baggage 13

   Import of firearms as baggage 14

   Export of gifts  14

   Import of gifts 15

   Regulation on vehicle registration in Delhi 16

   Reimport of car exported from India 19

   Car duty chart 19

   Baggage exemption for TR  19

   Documents for baggage 20

   Documents for commercial shipments 26

   Baggage rules 2016     26,27

   Transfer of residence rule 27,29,30

   - Items restricted by air, accompanied baggage, and cabin luggage. 11,42

   - Rules on baggage allowances and suitcase sizes. 11-12

7. **Foreign Trade Policy**

    o   Export of baggage. 12-13

    o   Import-export policies for specific items (e.g., firearms, gifts, cars). 12-13

8. **Car Import Policies**

    o   Car imports under transfer of residence.15

    o   Duty assessment charts and calculation specimens. 16-18

    o   Detailed car import policies. 47-58

9. **Special Circumstances**

    o   Export and import of pets. 20-23

    o   Baggage rules for deceased individuals.24-25

    o   Clearance and documentation for human remains.24-25

    o   Duty exemptions for government officials and foreign dignitaries.38-39

10. **Special Imports and Exports**

    o   Goods for repair abroad. 43

    o   Project-based imports and exports.43

    o   Prototype imports. 43

    o   Import through personal baggage 41

    o   Samples 41

    o   Personal effects 41

- Import of second-hand goods. 44

## 11. Diplomatic Exemptions 64

- Import-export policies for diplomats' personal effects and cars.

## 12. Authorized Import-Export Code (IEC) 45-47

- Categories and their applications. 45-47
- Documents and specimens for export of baggage by air 85-88
- Documents and specimens for export of baggage by sea 89-94

## 13. Exhibition Goods 68-70

## 14. Sale of exhibitions 70-72

## 15. Temporary Car Import Under Ata Carnet 17

## 16. Policy for import of vehicles 47-58

## 17. Courier 81

## 18. Weight calculation by air and sea 81

## 19. Additional tips 83

## 20. Packing guidelines 83

## 21. Survey for volume assessment 84

## 22. Baggage declaration forms

## 23. Tips for packing and shipment 79

## 24. Forign trade exemption from application of rules 59-78

25. Letters specimens for sea shipments Government officer 97-106

26. Additional tips 108

27. Specimen Air Way Bill 107

28. Specimen Sea way Bill , B/L 109

29. Shipping instructions sea and air 109-114

30. Contact information 115

31. Commercial shipments documents 26

32. Baggage rules 26

33. Transfer of residence rules 27-28

34. T R Exemption 29-30

35. Currency rules 30

36. Unaccompanied rules 29-30

37. Crew member 31

38. Exemption on certain items , annesure1 and 2  32

39. Special concession for foreign officials  33

40. TR for foreign National 34-35

41. Undertaking specimen for TR to foreigner 35-37

42. Export of gifts 14

43. Baggage examination 19

44. Documents required 19-20

# Contact Information

Ashok Khanna is available to provide detailed guidance and support for any related query. His practical approach, coupled with years of experience, ensures streamlined processes and compliance with all applicable rules and regulations.

For further assistance, reach out at Ashok@AshokaInt.com or Moving@AshokaInt.com.

# Policy Regarding Import/Export of Goods

## 1. General Policy (2.01 of Foreign Trade Policy)

- Export and import are **free** unless regulated through **prohibitions, restrictions**, or **exclusive trading** by State Trading Enterprises (STEs) as specified in the Indian Trade Classification (Harmonized System) [ITC (HS)].

- The list of prohibited, restricted, and STE items can be accessed under **Regulatory Updates**.

- Certain items may be free for trade but are subject to **conditions under other laws or acts**.

---

## 2. Baggage Rules (Ntfn 30 (NT), dated 01.03.2016)

### Definition

- Includes both **accompanied** and **unaccompanied** baggage.

### Allowances for Accompanied Baggage

- **Duty-Free Allowance:** ₹50,000 per person.
- **Liquor/Wine/Beer:** 2 litters per person.
- **Tobacco Products:**
    - 100 cigarettes
    - 25 cigars
    - 125 grams of tobacco

## Duty for Excess Items

- Cigarettes: ~153%
- Whisky: ~218%
- Wines/Beers: ~206%

---

## 3. Customs Clearance Channels

### Green Channel

- For passengers with no dutiable goods or items exceeding allowances.
- Customs checks may occur, and fines or duties may be applied if discrepancies are found.

### Red Channel

- For passengers declaring goods.
- Duties are assessed and payable at the counter.

**Note:** Free allowances cannot be pooled among passengers.

---

## 4. Transfer of Residence Rules

### Allowances Based on Duration Abroad

- **3-6 Months Stay:** ₹60,000 for personal/household goods (excluding Annexures I & II; including Annexure III).
- **1 Year Stay (preceding 2 years):** ₹2,00,000 (Mini Transfer of Residence).

- **2-Year Stay:** ₹5,00,000 under Transfer of Residence (with conditions):
  - Minimum stay of 2 years abroad before arrival.
  - Short visits to India not exceeding 6 months in 2 years.
  - Concession not availed in the preceding 3 years.

---

## 5. Relaxations

- Condition (i):
  - A shortfall of up to 2 months in the required stay abroad may be **condoned** by the Deputy/Assistant Commissioner of Customs under special circumstances (e.g., terminal leave or vacation).
  - Reasons must be documented in writing.

**Policy Regarding Import/Export of Goods (Continued)**

## 6. Relaxations

- **Condition (ii):**
  - Short visits exceeding 6 months during the 2-year period abroad may be condoned by the **Principal Commissioner of Customs** under special circumstances, with reasons recorded in writing.

---

## 7. Delay in Shipment of Unaccompanied Baggage

- **Time Limit for Dispatch:**

- o  By Air: 15 days after arrival in India.
- o  By Sea: 30 days after arrival in India.

- **Condonation for Delay:**
  - o  Customs may allow delays upon receiving valid reasons for late shipment.

---

## 8. Prohibited Items (Annexure I)

- **Firearms**
- **Cartridges:** More than 50 rounds.
- Tobacco Products: Exceeding 100 cigarettes, 25 cigars, or 125 grams of tobacco.
- Alcohol/Wine: Over 2 litters.
- Gold/Silver: In forms other than ornaments.
- Flat Panel Televisions: LCD, LED, Plasma.

---

## 9. Restricted Items (Annexure II)

- **Electronics and Appliances:**
  - o  Colour TV
  - o  Video home theatre system
  - o  Dishwasher
  - o  Deep freezer
  - o  Domestic refrigerator (above 300 litters)

- Video camera
- **Cinematographic Films**: 35mm and above.
- **Gold/Silver:** Non-ornamental forms.

---

## 10. Permissible Items (Annexure III)

- **Electronics and Appliances:**
  - Video cassette recorder
  - DVD player
  - Music system
  - Air conditioner
  - Microwave oven
  - Fax machine
  - Washing machine
  - Word processing machine
  - Portable photocopying machine
  - Gas cooking range
- **Computers:**
  - Desktop or laptop (notebook) computers.
- **Refrigerators:** Up to 300 litters.

---

## 11. Duty Rates

- **General Duty:**
  - 38.6% on items exceeding the free allowance under the **Baggage Rules, 2016.**

- **Unaccompanied Baggage:**
  - 16.5% duty for items not in Annexure III or any new items.
  - **CTV (Colour TV):** 38.5%.

- **Repeated Items from Annexure III:**
  - Duty: 38.5%.

---

## 12. Frequently Asked Questions (FAQs)

**Q: I am bringing items under Transfer of Residence. What will be the duty?**

**A: No duty applies to:**

- Video cassette recorder
- DVD player
- Music system
- Air conditioner
- Microwave oven
- Fax machine
- Washing machine
- Word processing machine

## 13. Additional Duty Information

- **Duty Rates for Specific Items:**
- **Color Television:** 38.6%
- **Video Home Theatre System:** 16.5%
- **Dishwasher:** 16.5%
- **Deep Freezer:** 16.5%
- **Domestic Refrigerator (above 300 liters):** 16.5%
- **Video Camera:** 16.5%
- **Repeated Items:**
- Duty: 38.6%
- **Exceptions (No Duty):**
- Firearms
- Firearm cartridges exceeding 50 rounds
- Tobacco products exceeding prescribed limits
- Goods imported via courier services.

---

## 14. Re-Import of Baggage

- Items previously exported from India can be re-imported without duty if returned within **3 years.**

---

## 15. Foodstuff by Foreigners

- Notification: 207 dated 17.07.1989
- Aggregate CIF value of foodstuff imports: **Up to ₹1,00,000/- per year.**
- Importer must use foreign currency from personal funds.

---

## 16. Laptop Computers

- **Notification**: 11 dated 08.01.2004
- **Laptops:** Duty-free for passengers aged 18 years or above.
- **Desktops:** Not included.

---

## 17. Jewelry Allowance

- For passengers residing abroad for **1+ years:**
- **Gentlemen:** 20 grams, value up to ₹50,000.
- **Ladies:** 40 grams, value up to ₹1,00,000.
- **Export of Gold Jewelry:**
- No value limit, but passengers are advised to obtain an **Export Certificate** at departure to avoid duty on return.

---

## 18. Export of Indian Currency

- Limit:
- Residents of India may carry up to ₹25,000 while traveling abroad.

---

## 19. Foreign Exchange for Travel

- Foreign exchange can be purchased from authorized dealers.
- Cash purchase limit: ₹50,000 or below.
- **20. Foreign Exchange Rules for Travel Abroad**
- **Carrying Foreign Currency:**
- Unlimited foreign currency can be carried by Indian residents when traveling abroad.
- **Currency Declaration Form (CDF):** Required if carrying:
- Foreign currency notes exceeding $5,000, or
- Total foreign exchange, including currency, exceeding $10,000.
- **Liberalized Remittance Scheme (LRS) Limit:**
- USD 2,50,000 per financial year for purposes such as:
- Private visits (excluding Nepal and Bhutan).
- Gifts or donations.

## 21. Restricted Items in Unaccompanied Baggage by Air

- Items not permitted without proper declarations include:

- **Household/Flammable Items:** Oil, ghee, shaving foam, perfumes, whisky, drone.

- **Electronic and Hazardous Items:** Battery, Bluetooth devices, magnets, radioactive materials.

- **Medicines and Substances:** Poisonous/infectious substances, narcotics.

- **Other Restricted Items:** Wildlife articles, antiques, foodstuffs.

## 22. Items Not Permitted in Hand Baggage

- Items disallowed include:

- **Sharp Objects:** Knives, blades, etc.

- **Liquids/Creams:** Cream lotions, alcohol, gels, liquids over **100 ml.**

- **Miscellaneous:** Spices, lotions.

## 23. Baggage Allowance by Air

- Checked Baggage:

- USA, Canada, Brazil: Two cases allowed.

- Size Limits:

- Economy Class: Up to 45 cubic inches, 20 kg.
- First Class: Up to 60 cubic inches, 40 kg.
- Business Class: Up to 30 cubic inches, 30 kg.
- Hand Baggage:
- Economy Class: 55x38x20 cm, 7 kg.
- Business Class: 12 kg.

---

## 24. Export of Passenger Baggage

- **Allowed Export:**
- Bonafide personal baggage may be exported:
- Along with the passenger.
- As unaccompanied baggage within one year before or after the passenger's departure.
- **Restrictions:**
- Items listed as restricted in the ITC HS code require authorization.
- **Special Provisions for Government Officials:**
- When traveling abroad for official postings, personal effects, including food items (free, restricted, or prohibited), are allowed for personal consumption under Customs Act, 1962.

## 25. Export of Freely Permissible Items as Baggage

- Items freely exported under **Foreign Trade Policy (FTP)** may also be exported as part of passenger baggage without requiring prior authorization.

---

## 26. Export of Commercial Goods as Baggage

- **Circular 17/95 Cus, dated 1.3.1995:**
- Export of goods by passengers as baggage is permitted if:
- The source of funds for purchasing the goods is foreign exchange brought by air passengers upon their arrival in India.
- Proper proof of procurement using foreign exchange is provided.
- Abuse of this provision must be reported to the Board with detailed cases.

---

## 27. Import of Firearms as Baggage

- **Strictly Prohibited:**
- Import of firearms and cartridges exceeding 50 rounds.
- Transfer of Residence (TR) Exception:
- **Firearms can be imported if:**
- They were in the passenger's possession and use abroad for at least one year.

- They will not be sold, loaned, or transferred during the importer's lifetime.
- The importer holds a valid arms license from local authorities.
- Applicable duties are paid.

---

## 28. Export of Gifts

- **Policy Guidelines (Para 2.32, FTP):**
- Goods, including edible items, up to **₹5,00,000** in value per licensing year, may be exported as gifts.
- Restricted items listed in **ITC (HS)** require authorization.

---

## 29. Import of Gifts

- Policy Guidelines (Para 2.26, FTP):
- Import of goods as gifts (e.g., via e-commerce, courier, or post) is prohibited, except for:
- **Life-saving medicines.**
- **Rakhi** (excluding other gifts related to Rakhi).
- **Duty-Free Limit:**
- Gifts valued up to ₹10,000 are duty-free under Notification 87/99 Cus, dated 6.7.1999.
- Gifts exceeding ₹10,000 are subject to applicable duty and fine.

## 30. Car Import Under Transfer of Residence (HS Code 87031090)

- **Eligibility Conditions:**
- Stay abroad for **2 years.**
- Visits to India must not exceed **180 days** in the last 2 years.
- Car ownership abroad for at least **1 year.**
- **Left-hand drive vehicles are not permitted.**
- **Required Documents:**
- Passport.
- Invoice.
- Old registration certificate showing 1-year ownership.

## 31. Regulations on Vehicle Registration in Delhi

- **Diesel Cars:** Vehicles older than **10 years** will not be registered.
- **Petrol Cars:** Vehicles older than **15 years** will not be registered.

## 32. Import Duty on Cars

- **Duty Rate: 204%** of CIF (Cost, Insurance, Freight) value.

- **Landing Charges:** 1% of CIF value.

---

## 33. Depreciation Allowance on Used Cars

- Depreciation is applied based on the car's age:
- **1 year old: 16%**
- **2 years old: 12%**
- **3 years old: 10%**
- **4 years old: 8%**
- **Maximum depreciation allowed: 70%**
- The final value of the car is often assessed by Chartered Engineers appointed by customs.

---

## 34. Re-Import of Cars Exported from India

- No duty is applicable if:
- No export incentives were claimed at the time of export.

---

## 35. Special Categories for Car Imports

- **Diplomatic Privileges:** Cars imported under diplomatic privileges are subject to special rules.
- **Temporary Imports:** Vehicles brought in under the **Carnet de Passages** system (temporary import permit) are allowed under specific conditions.

## 36. Duty Assessment Process

- When calculating duties for imported cars:

- **Ex-Factory Price:**

- Calculated as **(Value × 100)/114** after accounting for a **14% VAT**.

- Adjustments for:

- **Trade Discount:** e.g., 15% of value.

- **Depreciation:** As per age of the car.

- **Ad Hoc Depreciation Allowance:** If applicable.

- **Assessable Value:**

- FOB Value (Factory Price + Freight + Insurance).

- Add **Landing Charges:** 1% of CIF.

- **Duties:**

- **Import Duty:** 125%.

- **Integrated GST (IGST):** 28%.

- **Additional Duties (e.g., SGIS):** As applicable, typically 12.5%.

- **Total Effective Duty:** 204%.

- **Example Duty Assessment** (Car of Brand 'X')

- **Manufacture** Date: November 2004.

- The depreciation and other factors will determine the final assessable value.
- Duties and taxes (204% total) are then calculated on the adjusted CIF value.

## 37. Duty on Used Cars Under Transfer of Residence

- Example duty calculation for a 3-year-old car with an ex-factory price of ₹500,000:
- Ex-Factory Price (Including VAT): ₹500,000
- Less Trade Discount (15%): ₹75,000 → ₹425,000
- Less Depreciation (38%): ₹161,500 → ₹263,500
- FOB Value: ₹263,500
- Freight (20%): ₹52,700
- Insurance (1.125%): ₹3,557
- Landing Charges (1%): ₹3,098
- Net Assessable Value: ₹322,855
- Duty (204%): ₹658,624
- Final Note: This is an approximate calculation. Customs officers finalize duty upon inspection.

## 38. Baggage Examination for Transfer of Residence (TR)

- **Random Examination:** 10% of goods are randomly inspected (File No. 497/2/92 cus.vi, dated 08/04/93).

- **Discrepancy Found:** If discrepancies arise, **100% baggage** may be subject to inspection.
- **Non-TR Category:**
- All packages are examined.
- Duty: **36%** of assessed value.
- In Delhi, assessment for **non-bona fide baggage** is at ₹100/kg.

---

### 39. Documents Required for Baggage Clearance

- Passport
- Packing List
- Bill of Lading/Airway Bill
- Delivery Order (Issued by airline/shipping line)
- Authority Letter (If goods are cleared by an agent)
- Purchase Receipts (If available)
- PAN Card Copy (For Indians)
- Appointment Letter (For foreigners working in India)
- Duty Exemption Certificate (For diplomats, from MOFA)

---

### 40. Export of Pets

- Regulations and documents required for exporting pets:

- Examination by **Animal Quarantine and Certification Services (AQCS)**.
- **Veterinary Health Certificate** (Fit-to-fly by a registered vet).
- **Microchip Certificate**.
- **Vaccination Records**.
- **Passport Copy** (Owner).
- **Air Ticket Copy** (Owner).
- **Airway Bill** (If cargo transported).
- Authority Letter (If owner is unavailable).
- Specific import requirements (e.g., permits, tests).
- **Photographs:** Two 4x6-inch photos (light-facing).
- **IATA Standard Crate** (Mandatory for transport).
- Ensure compliance with import formalities of the destination country.

---

### 41. Notes on Pet Export

- **Documents Submission:** Submit self-attested originals and copies to AQCS at least 7 days before embarkation.
- **Vaccination Exceptions:** If the pet is too young, provide the mother's vaccination record.
- **Application:** Fill a separate form for each pet.

- Confirm appointments with AQCS before visiting.

---

## 42. Pet Relocation to India

- Plan and inform AQCS **3 months** before departure.
- Insert a **microchip** for identification.
- **Pet Relocation to India**
- **Advance Planning:** Notify authorities at least **3 months** before departure.
- **Microchip:** Insert a microchip for identification.
- **Vaccination Records:** Ensure all vaccinations are up-to-date and have records.
- **India Pet Health Certificate:** Obtain the certificate from a certified veterinarian.
- **Import Permit:** Secure the required import permit.
- **Dog License (For Dogs Only):** Mandatory for dogs.
- **IATA Standard Crate:** Required for safe transport.
- **Duty on Pets:**
- **38.5%** duty applicable.
- Value assessed between ₹10,000 to ₹20,000, depending on the breed and age.
- **No Duty on Exported and Reimported Pets:**
- Show original **export documents** to avail of this exemption.

**Baggage of Deceased Persons**

- **Allowance:**
- Personal and household goods belonging to the deceased are allowed **duty-free**.
- **Conditions:**
- Submit a **certificate** from the **Indian Embassy/High Commission** confirming ownership of the goods by the deceased person.
- Embassy may also attest the **packing list** for the goods.

**Clearance of Human Remains**

- Required Documents for Clearance in Delhi:
- No Objection Letter & Death Certificate:
- Issued by the Indian Embassy.
- Death Certificate:
- Issued by the local government office with the cause of death specified.
- Health Department Letter:
- Confirms that the death was not due to infectious diseases.
- Funeral Director Letter:

- Certifies the coffin is hermetically sealed and arterially embalmed.

- Embalming Certificate:

- Confirms proper embalming of the body.

- Cancelled Passport:

- Copy of the deceased person's cancelled passport.

- Consignee Details:

- Include the mobile number of the person in India who will be present at clearance.

- Airway Bill Copy:

- Required for clearance at New Delhi.

- Mortal Remains Clearance

- Documents:

- All original documents and cancelled passport must accompany the mortal remains.

- Passport cancellation by Immigration authorities and clearance from a Health Officer are mandatory.

- Facilitation:

- Airlines typically assist in completing the necessary formalities.

- Approach the Indian Freight Officer (IFO) at the Import Shed, Air Cargo Complex, for release of remains.

- IFO operates 24/7 to ensure smooth processing.

**Commercial Shipments Documentation**

- Invoice
- Packing List
- Import Export Number
- GST Number
- Bank Authorized Code Number
- Cross-cancelled Cheque and PAN Card (if not registered with customs).
- Authority Letter
- Import License (if applicable).

**Baggage Rules 2016 (Duty-Free Exemptions)**

- General Exemptions:
- Eligibility:
- Indian residents, foreigners residing in India, and tourists (excluding infants).
- Arriving from countries other than Nepal, Bhutan, and Myanmar.
- Duty-Free Allowance:
- Personal effects and souvenirs (used items).
- Articles (not listed in Annexure-I) up to ₹50,000 in value.

- Infants: Only used personal effects allowed duty-free.
- From Nepal, Bhutan, and Myanmar:
- Duty-Free Allowance:
- Personal effects and souvenirs (used items).
- Articles (not in Annexure-I) up to ₹15,000 in value.
- Infants: Only used personal effects allowed duty-free.
- Jewellery Exemptions:
- Passengers residing abroad for over 1 year:
- Gentlemen: Jewellery up to 20g and ₹50,000 in value.
- Ladies: Jewellery up to 40g and ₹1,00,000 in value.

---

**Transfer of Residence (TR) Rules**

- Eligibility:
- Engaged in a profession abroad or transferring residence to India.
- Allowed additional duty-free articles as per the appendix.
- Conditions:
- Must meet specific eligibility criteria in column (3) of the appendix.
- Some conditions may be relaxed, as per column (4) of the appendix.

---

Notes:

- These rules aim to streamline passenger and cargo processing while ensuring compliance with customs regulations.

- For assistance, individuals should approach customs officers, airline representatives, or relevant government departments for clarifications.

- **Summary of Appendix and Additional Rules for Baggage and Currency:**

---

## Transfer of Residence (TR) Exemptions (Appendix):

| Duration of Stay Abroad | Articles Allowed Free of Duty | Conditions | Relaxations |
|---|---|---|---|
| 3 to 6 Months | Personal and household articles (excluding Annexures I & II, including Annexure III) up to ₹60,000. | Indian passenger. | None. |
| 6 Months to 1 Year | Personal and household articles (excluding Annexures I & II, including Annexure III) up to ₹1,00,000. | Indian passenger. | None. |
| 1 Year (During Previous 2 Years) | Personal and household articles (excluding Annexures I & II, including Annexure III) up to ₹2,00,000. | No concession availed in the preceding 3 years. | None. |
| 2 Years or More | Personal and household articles (excluding Annexures I & II, including Annexure III) up to ₹5,00,000. | - Minimum 2 years abroad immediately before arrival. | |

- Short visits (≤6 months) in 2 years prior are permitted.

- No concession availed in the preceding 3 years. | - **Condition (i):** Up to 2-month shortfall in stay abroad can be condoned if:

  a) Terminal leave/vacation.

  b) Special circumstances (recorded in writing).

- **Condition (ii):** Principal Commissioner of Customs may condone excess short visits >6 months in special cases (with recorded reasons). |

---

## Currency Rules:

- Governed by Foreign Exchange Management (Export and Import of Currency) Regulations, 2015.
- Refer to relevant regulations and notifications for specific details.

---

## Unaccompanied Baggage Rules:

- Applicability:
- These rules cover unaccompanied baggage unless specifically excluded.
- Dispatch and Timing:
- Baggage must have been in possession of the passenger abroad.
- It should be dispatched within 1 month of arrival in India or a further period approved by Customs authorities.

- Pre-arrival Landing:
- Baggage may arrive up to 2 months before the passenger.
- Extensions (up to 1 year) may be granted if:
- Delays occurred due to illness, natural calamities, disrupted travel arrangements, or other uncontrollable circumstances.
- Further Details on Baggage and Concessions for Crew Members and Trade Officials:

---

**Crew Members:**

- Baggage Importation:
- These rules apply to crew members of foreign-going conveyances when their employment ends, allowing them to bring in their personal baggage.
- Petty Gift Items:
- Crew members may bring items such as chocolates, cheese, cosmetics, and other small gifts for personal or family use.
- The total value of such goods should not exceed ₹1,500.

---

**Exemptions for Certain Articles (Annexure-I and II):**

- **Annexure I**: Items such as:

- **Firearms** and **ammunition** (exceeding specified limits).
- **Cigarettes**, **cigars**, and **tobacco** (exceeding specified quantities).
- **Alcoholic beverages** (exceeding 2 liters).
- **Gold/Silver** (other than ornaments).
- **Flat Panel Televisions** (LCD, LED, or Plasma).
- **Annexure II**: Items such as:
- **Colour Televisions**.
- **Video Home Theatre Systems**.
- **Domestic Refrigerators** (over 300 liters).
- **Gold/Silver** (other than ornaments).

---

**Personal Household Effects (Annexure III):**

- Household Goods and Electronics: Items like air conditioners, microwave ovens, personal computers, washing machines, and refrigerators up to 300 liters can be imported free of duty under specified rules.
- The list also includes music systems, fax machines, and laptop computers.

---

**Special Concessions for Foreign Officials:**

- Concessions for Trade Officials:

- Personal and household effects, including motor vehicles, are allowed duty-free for Trade Commissioners, Trade Representatives, or Trade Agents from foreign or Commonwealth countries, as well as their families.

- Official Goods: Items imported for the official use of these officers (including motor vehicles) can also be cleared duty-free.

- Special Rules for Imported Samples:

- Samples (such as advertising materials) imported by foreign officials for display or distribution are exempt, provided they are produced in the officer's home country and for office use.

- Corresponding Exemptions for Indian Officers:

- Indian officials of similar rank should receive corresponding exemptions, provided they meet the same criteria outlined by the Foreign Privileged Person (Regulation of Customs Privileges) Rules, 1957.

**Transfer of Residence for Foreign Nationals - Updated Guidelines for Customs Clearance**

**Background:**

Under Notification 27 dated 31.03.2016, individuals on **Bonafide transfer of residence** to India are entitled to transfer their personal baggage duty-free. However, there have been challenges and delays in the clearance process for foreign nationals, especially with regards to the documentation required.

**Recent Developments:**

1. **Grievances from Foreign Nationals:**

    - **Embassy of Japan,** New Delhi, and other logistics companies raised concerns that additional documents, particularly **proof of address**, were being requested by customs officers at certain stations.

    - This led to delays and confusion, as the required documentation was already listed in **Public Notice No. 145/2016** dated **04.11.2016**.

2. **Clarification on Documentation:**

    - It has been clarified that foreign nationals who are transferring their residence to India under a **work visa or authorization** issued by the **Ministry of External Affairs** are considered to have undergone the necessary **antecedent verification** by the respective Ministry.

    - Therefore, **proof of address** will **not** be required for these foreign nationals at customs clearance.

    - Instead, the customs officers will require:

        o **An undertaking from the employer** confirming the genuineness of the employee's details.

        o **An undertaking from the foreign national** regarding compliance with the **Customs Act, 1962** in case of any violations.

3. **Continued Documentation Submission:**

   - **All other documents** mentioned in **Public Notice No. 145/2016** will continue to be required. These include:

     o Passport and visa details.

     o Packing list and details of baggage.

     o Other supporting documents as per customs requirements.

4. **Effective Date:**

   - These instructions are **effective immediately** and will continue until further notice.

Office Of The Pr. Commissioner Of Customs, Ns-I
Jawaharlal Nehru Customs House, Nhava Sheva,
Tal-Uran, District-Raigad, Maharashtra-400 707
E-Mail Id:- Ubc-Jnch@Gov.In

F.NO.S/43-Misc-12/2021-22/UBC/JNCH
Date: 06.08.2024

## Office Note

**Subject: - Documents to be submitted by foreign passengers for clearance of Baggage at UB Centre, JNCH-reg.**

Attention of staff posted at the Unaccompanied Baggage Centre, JNCH is drawn towards the challenges encountered by the foreign Nationals, during clearance of their unaccompanied baggage.

2. There have been recent grievances and request raised by the Embassy of Japan, New Delhi and other logistics companies for clarification and facilitation of Customs Clearance for foreign nationals. It has come to the Notice that additional documents are being asked by Customs officers in addition to the documents mentioned in Public Notice No. 145/2016 dated 04.11.2016 especially related to the proof of address.

3. The matter has been examined. Since, the foreign nationals are transferring their residence to India on the basis of the work visa/authorization issued by the Ministry of External Affairs, it is imperative to presume that the antecedent verification of the said foreign nationals have already been

completed by the respective Ministry. Thus, the proof of residence for the said foreign nationals coming to India on work visa/authorization need not be asked for by the UBC officers. Instead, only an undertaking from the employer for the genuineness of the employee details and undertaking of the foreign National in India in case of any violations of Customs Act, 1962 may be taken from them. All the other documents mentioned in Public Notice No. 145/2016 dated 04.11.2016 as being submitted by the CHA/foreign passengers will continue to be submitted as per the current practice.

4. These instructions shall come into effect immediately and until further orders.

Sd/-

Jay G. Waghmare

Joint Commissioner of Customs

UBC, JNCH, NHAVA SHEVA

**Exemption of Articles of Gift and Goods from Customs Duty and Integrated Tax for Specific Individuals**

## 1. Exemption for Articles of Gift - Notification No. 326 dated 23.12.1983 (as amended)

**Purpose**: This notification provides exemptions from customs duties and integrated taxes for articles of gift received by government officials and foreign dignitaries, subject to certain conditions.

- **Exemptions:**
    - The whole of the duty of customs as per the Customs Tariff Act, 1975.
    - The whole of the integrated tax under section 3(7) of the Customs Tariff Act.

- **Eligibility:**
    - **Persons receiving gifts from foreign governments**: If they belong to any class specified in the schedule and are importing the gift as part of their baggage.
    - **Foreign dignitaries visiting India**: They are allowed to bring gifts for individuals listed in the schedule, as part of their baggage.

- **Conditions:**
    - The recipient must make a declaration to the Assistant Commissioner or Deputy Commissioner of Customs.
    - Foreign dignitaries must declare that the gifts are meant for specified individuals and are part of their official baggage.

**The Schedule:**

- **Ministers** of the Union, State, or Union Territory.

- **Persons in public service** related to the affairs of the Union or State, excluding those employed by government-owned corporations.

---

**2. Exemption from Integrated Tax for Baggage - Notification No. 183 dated 01.03.1986**

**Purpose:** This notification exempts integrated taxes on goods brought into India by passengers or crew members as part of their baggage.

- **Exemption:**
  - All goods falling under **heading No. 98.03** of the Customs Tariff Act are exempt from the whole of the integrated tax when imported as baggage.

---

**3. Exemption for Goods Imported or Purchased by the Vice-President of India - Notification No. 36 dated 30.06.2017**

**Purpose:** This notification exempts certain goods imported or purchased out of bond by the **Vice-President of India** from customs duties and integrated taxes.

- **Exemptions:**
  - Goods specified in **Column (2)** of the table below are exempt from:
    - **Customs duties** as per the First Schedule to the Customs Tariff Act.

- **Integrated tax** and **Goods and Services Tax compensation cess** as per sections 3(7) and 3(9) of the Customs Tariff Act.

**Exempt Goods:**

- **Articles for personal use**: Items used by the Vice-President or any member of their family.

- **Food, drink, and tobacco**: For consumption by the Vice-President's household or guests, official or otherwise.

- **Furnishings**: For any of the Vice-President's official residences.

- **Motor cars**: Provided for the Vice-President's personal use.

- **Effective Date**: This notification came into force on **1st July 2017**.

These notifications provide various customs duty exemptions to foreign dignitaries, government officials, and the Vice-President of India, ensuring smoother customs procedures and facilitating official activities.

## Import through Passenger Baggage - Baggage Rules and Conditions

### 1. Import of Household Goods and Personal Effects

- **Bona-fide household goods and personal effects** may be imported as part of passenger baggage, provided they comply with the limits, terms, and conditions outlined in the **Baggage Rules** as notified by the Ministry of Finance.

## 2. Import of Samples

- **Samples of freely importable items**: Samples that are freely importable under the **Foreign Trade Policy (FTP)** may be imported as part of passenger baggage without the need for an authorization. The import must comply with the conditions of the **Baggage Rules** as notified by Customs from time to time.

## 3. Import by Exporters

- **Exporters returning from abroad** are allowed to import items such as **drawings, patterns, labels, price tags, buttons, belts, trimming, and embellishments** required for export purposes, as part of their passenger baggage. This is allowed without the need for an authorization, subject to the value limit specified in the **FTP** or as per the relevant Customs notifications.

## 4. Import of Restricted or Prohibited Items

- **Restricted, prohibited, or canalized items**: Any item(s), including samples or prototypes, whose import policy is "restricted" or "prohibited" or is canalized through **State Trading Enterprises (STEs)** are **not permitted** as part of passenger baggage unless the passenger holds a valid authorization or permission from the **Directorate General of Foreign Trade (DGFT)**.

**Key Takeaways:**

- **Household goods** and **personal effects** can be imported as baggage within limits set by the **Baggage Rules**.

- **Freely importable samples** and materials for **exporters** can also be brought in as part of baggage without needing additional authorization.

- **Restricted or prohibited items** require proper authorization from **DGFT** to be imported through baggage.

These provisions are in place to ensure that imports through passenger baggage

## 2.28 Re–import of goods repaired abroad

Capital goods, equipment, components, parts and accessories, whether imported or indigenous, except those restricted under ITC (HS) may be sent abroad for repairs, testing, quality improvement or upgradation or standardization or technology and re-imported without and Authorization.

## 2.29 Import of goods used in projects abroad

Project contractors after completion of projects abroad, may import without an Authorization, goods including capital goods used in the project, provided they have been used for at least one year.

## 2.30 Import of Prototypes

Import of new/second hand prototypes/second hand samples may be allowed on payment of duty without an Authorization to an Actual User (Industrial) engaged in production of or having industrial license/letter of intent for research in item for which prototype is sought for product development or research, as the case may be, upon a self-declaration to that effect, to the satisfaction of Customs authorities.

## Import policy for Second Hand Goods:

## 2.31 Second Hand Goods

| Sl. No. | Categories of Second-Hand Goods | Import Policy | Conditions, If any |
|---|---|---|---|
| I. | **Second Hand Capital Goods** | | |
| I(a) | I. Desktop Computers; | Restricted | Importable against |

Public Notice No. 09/2015-20 (Dated 29 June 2017)

**Government of India** Ministry of Commerce & Industry
Department of Commerce
Directorate General of Foreign Trade
Udyog Bhawan, New Delhi - 110 011

---

**Subject: Modification in para 2.07 (b) of Handbook of Procedure (2015-2020)**

In exercise of powers conferred under paragraph 2.04 of the Foreign Trade Policy (2015-2020), the Director General of Foreign Trade (DGFT) hereby modifies para 2.07(b) of the Handbook of Procedure – IEC Number Exempted Categories as follows:

The following permanent **IEC (Import Export Code)** numbers shall be used by **non-commercial PSUs** and specific categories of importers/exporters for import/export purposes:

| Sr. No. | Existing Permanent IEC | Revised Permanent IEC Numbers | Categories of Importer/Exporter |
|---|---|---|---|
| 1 | 0100000011 | AMDCG0111E | All Ministers/Departments of Central Government and agencies wholly or partially owned by them. |
| 2 | 0100000029 | ADSGA0129E | All Ministers/Departments of any State Government and agencies wholly or partially owned by them. |
| 3 | 0100000037 | DCUNO0137E | Diplomatic personnel, consular officers in India, and officials of UNO and its specialized agencies. |
| 4 | 0100000045 | IABBR0145E | Indian nationals returning from/going abroad and claiming benefits under the **Baggage Rules**. |
| 5 | 0100000053 | IIHIE0153E | Persons/Institutions/Hospitals importing/exporting goods for personal use, not related to trade, manufacture, or agriculture. |
| 6 | 0100000061 | IIEGN0161E | Persons importing/exporting goods from/to **Nepal**. |
| 7 | 0100000070 | IIEGM0170E | Persons importing/exporting goods from/to **Myanmar** through Indo-Myanmar border areas. |
| 8 | ~ | IIEGB0180E | Persons importing/exporting goods from/to **Bhutan**. |

| Sr. No. | Existing Permanent IEC | Revised Permanent IEC Numbers | Categories of Importer/Exporter |
|---|---|---|---|
| 9 | 0100000096 | ATAEF1096E | Importers bringing goods for display or use in fairs/exhibitions under the provisions of the **ATA carnet**. |
| 10 | 0100000100 | IDNBG1100E | Director, **National Blood Group**. |
| 11 | 0100000126 | ICIRN1126E | Individuals/Charitable Institutions/NGOs importing goods exempt from customs duty for use by victims affected by natural calamities. |
| 12 | 0100000134 | IIEGC1134E | Persons importing/exporting permissible goods from/to **China** through Gunji, Namgaya Shipkila, and Nathula ports, subject to value ceilings of single consignment. |
| 13 | 0100000169 | NCIEE1169E | Non-commercial imports and exports by entities authorized by **Reserve Bank of India**. |

**Effect of Public Notice:**

- The revised **permanent IEC numbers** listed above are effective **from 1st July 2017**. These revisions are made to migrate to the **alpha-numeric format** for IEC numbers.

**Policy on Import of Vehicles in India: Comprehensive Guidelines**

## Definitions and Key Terms

- **Second-Hand or Used Vehicles**: A vehicle is classified as second-hand or used if it:
  - Has been **sold, leased, or loaned** prior to importation into India, or
  - Has been **registered for use** in another country prior to its importation.

- **New Imported Vehicles**: A vehicle is considered new if:
  - It has not been manufactured or assembled in India,
  - It has not been sold, leased, or loaned before importation, and
  - It has not been registered for use in any country prior to importation.

---

## Conditions for Importing Second-Hand or Used Vehicles

- **Vehicle Age:**
  - The vehicle must not be older than **three years** from the date of manufacture.

- **Design and Safety Standards:**
  - The vehicle must:
    - Have **right-hand steering** and controls (except for two- or three-wheelers),

- Include a **speedometer** calibrated in kilometers, and
- Feature **headlamp photometry** suitable for "keep left" traffic systems.

- **Compliance with Indian Laws:**
  - The vehicle must conform to the **Motor Vehicles Act, 1988**, and the associated rules.

- **Import Certification Requirements:**
  - Importers must:
    - Provide a certificate from a notified testing agency confirming that the vehicle was tested before shipment and complies with the **Motor Vehicles Act, 1988**.
    - Submit a certificate from the same testing agency affirming compliance with the original **homologation certificate** issued during manufacturing.
    - Submit the vehicle for testing upon arrival in India at one of the approved agencies (e.g., Automotive Research Association of India, Pune).

- **Port Restrictions:**
  - Second-hand or used vehicle imports are permitted only through the **Mumbai customs port**.

- **Roadworthiness and Service Commitment:**
  - The vehicle must have a minimum **roadworthiness period of five years** from the date of importation.
  - Importers must assure **service facilities** for the vehicle within India during this period.
  - A declaration and supporting certificate regarding roadworthiness must be submitted during importation.

- **Exemption for Vintage Cars:**
  - Vehicles manufactured before **January 1, 1950**, are free for import by **Actual Users** and exempt from the above conditions.
  - Such vehicles must comply with the **Motor Vehicles Act, 1988** if used on public roads.

---

Conditions for Importing New Vehicles

- **Definition:**
  - A new vehicle must:
    - Not have been manufactured or assembled in India,
    - Not have been previously sold, leased, or loaned,
    - Not have been registered for use in any country prior to importation.

- **Import Requirements for New Vehicles:**
    - To be detailed based on the continuation of the policy. (Let me know if you need the rest of this policy elaborated.)

**Detailed Guidelines on Import of New Vehicles in India**

**Conditions for Importing New Vehicles**

- **Design and Safety Standards:**
    - The vehicle must:
        - Have a speedometer calibrated in kilometers per hour (km/h).
        - Feature right-hand steering and controls (applicable to vehicles other than two- and three-wheelers).
        - Have headlamp photometry designed for "keep-left" traffic systems.
        - Be imported from the country of manufacture. The term "country of manufacture" also includes a unified market like the European Union (EU).

- **Compliance with Indian Laws:**
    - The vehicle must meet all the provisions of the **Motor Vehicles Act, 1988**, and the rules applicable on the date of importation.

- **Importer Responsibilities:**
    - The importer or dealer must:

- Hold a valid **Certificate of Compliance** as per Rule 126 of the **Central Motor Vehicle Rules (CMVR), 1989**, for the model being imported.
- Fulfill all obligations assigned to the manufacturer under **Rules 122 and 138 of CMVR, 1989**, including issuing **Form 22**.
- Submit proof of compliance with **Rule 126A of CMVR** regarding conformity of production within **six months** of the import. Failure to do so will result in a ban on further imports of that vehicle model.

- **Authorized Customs Ports for Import:**
  - Imports are permitted only through designated **customs ports**:
    - **Seaports**: Nhava Sheva, Mumbai, Kolkata, Chennai, Ennore, Cochin, Katupalli, APM Terminals Pipavav, Krishnapatnam, Vishakhapatnam.
    - **Airports**: Mumbai Air Cargo Complex, Delhi Air Cargo, Chennai Airport.
    - **Inland Container Depots (ICDs)**: Talegaon Pune, Tughlakabad, Faridabad.

- **Exemptions:**
  - The provisions do not apply to imports of vehicles for:
    - Certification under Rule 126 of CMVR.

- Defense purposes.
  - **R&D Vehicles:**
    - Vehicle and auto component manufacturers can import new vehicles for **research and development (R&D)**.
    - These vehicles cannot be registered under CMVR and cannot ply on Indian roads. Necessary endorsements are made by customs at the time of clearance.
- **Special Provisions for Landlocked Countries:**
  - If the country of manufacture is landlocked and the shipment is made from another country, the vehicle will be considered exported from the country of manufacture, provided supporting documentation traces the shipment route.

---

**Exemptions from Conditions for Specific Categories of Importers**

Certain importers can import passenger cars, jeeps, multi-utility vehicles, etc., on payment of full customs duty without adhering to the general conditions:

- **Individuals:**
  - Returning to India for permanent settlement after **two years of continuous stay abroad**, provided the vehicle has been in their possession for **at least one year** abroad.

- **Award Recipients:**
    - Indian residents presented with a vehicle as an award in any **international event, match, or competition.**

- **Legal Heirs:**
    - Legal heirs or successors of deceased relatives residing abroad.

- **Physically Handicapped Persons:**
    - Allowed to import vehicles for personal use.

- **Corporate Entities:**
    - Companies incorporated in India with **foreign equity participation.**

- **Branches/Offices of Foreign Firms:**
    - Allowed to import vehicles for official use.

- **Charitable/Religious Institutions:**
    - Institutions registered under relevant laws and functioning for community benefit can import vehicles, subject to clearance under the **Foreign Contribution (Regulation) Act, 1976.**

- **Honorary Consuls:**
    - Foreign Honorary Consuls on recommendation by the **Ministry of External Affairs.**

- **Foreign Journalists:**
    - Journalists and correspondents accredited with the Press Information Bureau, Ministry of Information and Broadcasting.

## Additional Conditions and Exemptions for Vehicle Imports

### 1. General Conditions for Imports with Specific Categories

- **Right-Hand Steering and Controls:**
    - All imported vehicles (other than two- and three-wheelers) must have **right-hand steering and controls**.

- **Entitlement for Vehicle Imports:**
    - Categories (e) and (f) are allowed to import a **maximum of three vehicles**.
    - Categories (a) to (d) and (g) to (i) can import only **one vehicle**.
    - Physically handicapped persons (category d) may import only **specially designed vehicles** suitable for their use.

- **Restriction on Sale:**
    - Imported vehicles carry a **"NO SALE" condition for two years**, enforced by Customs and Regional Transport Authorities during registration.

- **Relaxations:**
  - The **Director General of Foreign Trade (DGFT)** may relax these conditions for special circumstances or categories not listed above.

---

## 2. Bonds/Bank Guarantees for Pre-1997 Imports

- Bonds or bank guarantees executed before **March 31, 1997**, for vehicles not transferred, are deemed **discharged as of March 31, 2000**, per Public Notice No. 3 (RE-2000)/97-02.

---

## 3. Exemptions for Foreign Diplomats and Privileged Persons

- Foreign diplomats and other privileged persons exempt from customs duties are also exempt from the conditions in **Sections 1 and 2**.

- Disposal of such vehicles is regulated under the **Foreign Privileged Persons (Regulation of Customs Privileges) Rules, 1957**.

---

## 4. Broadcasting and Specialty Vehicles

- **DSNG Vans/OB Vans:**
  - Exempt from conditions in **Sections 1 and 2**, provided they have **right-hand steering and controls**.

- **All-Terrain Vehicles (ATVs):**
  - ATVs used for off-road sports, recreation, or farming are exempt from **Sections 1 and 2** as they are not subject to **Central Motor Vehicles Rules (CMVR)** registration.

---

## 5. High-Value New Vehicle Imports

- **Vehicles with:**
  - FOB value ≥ USD 40,000, and
  - Engine capacity > 3000cc for petrol or > 2500cc for diesel,
- Can be imported by individuals, companies, or OEMs, exempting conditions in:
  - **Section 2(II)(a)(iv)**: Origin of shipment from the manufacturing country.
  - **Section 2(II)(c)**: Local testing requirements.
- Requirements:
  - At customs clearance, submit a Type Approval Certificate/Certificate of Conformity (COP) from an accredited agency, complying with ECE regulations or the EU Directive.

---

## 6. Vehicles Imported for Jobbing and Re-Export

- New or second-hand vehicles (not older than three years from manufacture) are exempt from **Section**

2(II)(c) for jobbing and subsequent **re-export** under **Customs Notification No. 32/97 CUS (N.T.)**.

---

## 7. Special Rules for Motorcycles

- Motorcycles with engine capacity ≥ 800cc are exempt from Section 2(II)(c).

- Requirements:

  o Submit a **Type Approval Certificate/Certificate of COP** from an EU-accredited agency, specifying compliance with:

    - **EU Directive 168/2013/EU** (technical and emission standards),

    - **EURO IV** norms (test procedure under Regulation EU No. 134/2014).

- Transitional Provisions for EURO III Norms:

  o Motorcycles meeting **EURO III** standards (EU Directive 2003/77/EC) were exempt until **March 31, 2017**.

  o These imports required the submission of compliance certificates referencing **EU Directive 2002/24/EC**.

**Foreign Trade (Exemption from Application of Rules in Certain Cases) Order, 1993**

**Issued by the Ministry of Commerce (Director General of Foreign Trade)**

**Date of Order:** 31st December 1993
**Notification Number:** S.O. 1056(E)

---

### 1. Short Title and Commencement

- This order is named the Foreign Trade (Exemption from Application of Rules in Certain Cases) Order, 1993.

- It becomes effective on the date of its publication in the Official Gazette.

---

### 2. Definitions

For the purposes of this order:

- "Act": Refers to the Foreign Trade (Development and Regulation) Act, 1992 (22 of 1992).

- "Import Trade Regulations": Includes:

  o The **Act**, rules, and orders made under it.

  o The export and import policy.

- "Rules": Denotes the Foreign Trade (Regulation) Rules, 1993.

- Words and expressions not defined in this order but defined in the **Act** will have the meanings assigned to them under the **Act**.

---

## 3. Exemptions from the Application of Rules

The provisions of the **Foreign Trade (Regulation) Rules, 1993**, will **not apply** to the import of goods under the following circumstances:

### (a) Imports by the Central Government or its agencies:

- Goods imported for **defense purposes** by the Central Government or undertakings owned and controlled by it.

### (b) Imports through Government purchase organizations:

- Imports by:
    - Central or State Governments.
    - Statutory corporations or public bodies.
    - Government undertakings operated as joint-stock companies.
- **Orders must be placed via:**
- India Supply Mission, London, or
- India Supply Mission, Washington.

### (c) Imports coordinated by the Directorate General of Supplies and Disposals (DGS&D):

- **Imports by:**
    - Central or State Governments.

- o Statutory corporations, public bodies, or government undertakings operating as joint-stock companies.
- Orders coordinated through the **DGS&D, New Delhi**.

(d) **Transshipment or bonded goods:**

- **Goods that are:**
- **Transhipped** through India or bonded upon arrival for **re-export** as ship stores to countries (excluding Nepal and Bhutan).
- Released for **diplomatic personnel, consular officers**, and **United Nations officials** exempt from duty under:
    - Notification No. 3, dated 8th January 1957 (Ministry of Finance).
    - The United Nations (Privileges and Immunities) Act, 1947.

(e) **Duty-Free Shop Imports:**

- Goods imported and bonded on arrival for sale at **approved duty-free shops**:
    - o For outgoing or incoming passengers.
    - o Payment must be made in **free foreign exchange**.

(f) **Goods in transit:**

- Goods in transit through India:

- By post or otherwise to destinations outside India (except Nepal and Bhutan).
- Must remain in the custody of **postal** or **customs authorities** while in India.

**(g) Goods transmitted across India:**

- **Goods sent:**
  - By air to **Afghanistan**.
  - By land to countries (other than Nepal and Bhutan).
- These imports are exempt from duty or qualify for duty refunds, provided:
  - The importer undertakes to produce evidence within a specified period that the goods have crossed India's borders.
  - Failure to comply may result in a penalty.

---

**Additional Conditions**

- Goods imported under exemptions must meet specific requirements, such as:
  - Being under the custody of customs or postal authorities while in India.
  - Importers providing valid documentation or evidence as required.
- Penalties may be imposed for failure to comply with these conditions or requirements.

**Additional Conditions and Provisions for Import Exemptions**

**Exemptions Under Specific Circumstances**

**(h) Passenger Baggage**

- **General Allowance:**

    o Goods imported as **passenger baggage** are exempt to the extent permissible under the **Baggage Rules**, except for:

        - **Quinine** exceeding:
        - 500 tablets, or
        - 1/3 lb. powder, or
        - 100 ampoules.

- **Tourist Obligations:**

    o Articles of high value imported by a **tourist** under Rule 7 of the **Tourist Baggage Rules, 1978**, must be re-exported upon their departure.

    o Failure to re-export will result in the goods being considered **prohibited imports** under the **Customs Act, 1962 (52 of 1962)**.

**Gold Importation:**

- Passengers of **Indian origin** or holding a valid passport under the **Passports Act, 1967 (15 of 1967)** can import gold as baggage under these conditions:

    o The passenger has stayed abroad for a minimum of **six months**.

- The imported gold must not exceed **5 kilograms per passenger**.
- **Import duty** must be paid in **convertible foreign currency**.
- No restrictions apply on the **sale** of imported gold.

---

### (i) Personal Use or Institutional Imports

- **Exemptions:**
  - Imports made **via post** or otherwise for **personal use** or by institutions/hospitals are exempt, except for:
    - **Vegetable seeds** exceeding 1 lb.
    - **Bees**.
    - **Tea**.
    - Literature restricted under the current **policy**.
    - Goods **canalized** under the policy.
    - **Alcoholic beverages**.
    - **Firearms and ammunition**.
    - Consumer **electronic items** (except **hearing aids** and **life-saving equipment**).

### CIF Value Limitation:

- The **Cost, Insurance, and Freight (CIF)** value of goods imported at one time must not exceed ₹2,000.

## (j) Diplomatic Imports

- Imports by or on behalf of **diplomatic personnel, consular officers**, and **trade commissions** in India are exempt if duty is waived under:

  - **Notification No. 3**, dated **8th January 1957** (Ministry of Finance, Department of Revenue).

---

## (k) Re-Imported Goods

- Goods from any country are exempt from Customs duty on re-importation under various **notifications**, such as:

  - Notification Nos. 113 (16 May 1957), 103 (25 March 1958), and others.

  - Applies specifically to goods exempted through earlier notifications regarding re-imports.

---

## (l) Goods for Repair and Re-Export

- **Indian-manufactured goods** or **foreign parts** exported and re-imported by manufacturers for repair and re-export are exempt, provided:

  - Customs authorities verify that the re-imported goods are the same as those exported.

  - For goods not exempted under **Customs Notification No. 132 (9 December 1961)**:

- The importer must execute a **bond** stating that the goods will be re-exported after repair within **six months**.

---

### (m) Imports by UN Officials

- Officials of the **United Nations Organization** and its specialized agencies are exempt from payment of Customs duty.

---

### Summary of Key Provisions

- Passenger baggage is generally exempt within prescribed limits, with special rules for gold imports and obligations for high-value articles by tourists.

- Personal-use imports and institutional goods have specific exemptions with clear limitations.

- Re-imported goods, diplomatic goods, and UN-related imports benefit from unique exemptions and conditions.

- Goods for repair and re-export have specific procedural requirements for customs verification and bond execution.

### Additional Exemptions from Customs Duty and Application of Rules

### Exemptions Under the United Nations (Privileges and Immunities) Act, 1947

### (n) Imports by the Ford Foundation:

- Goods imported by the **Ford Foundation** are exempt from customs duty as per the agreement between the **Government of India** and the **Ford Foundation**.

(o) **Temporary Importation of Vehicles and Parts:**

- Vehicles or their components as defined in the Customs Convention on the Temporary Importation of Private Road Vehicles are exempt under Notification No. 296 dated 2nd August 1976, provided:

  o The vehicles or parts are **re-exported** within the specified period or an extended period granted by customs authorities.

  o No provisions of the notification or the associated **"Triptyque or Carnet-De-Passage" permit** are violated.

---

## EXHINITBITS

### 2.60 Import/Export of Exhibits for National and International Exhibitions/Fairs

(a) **Temporary Import/Export of Exhibits:**

- Import or export of exhibits, including construction and decorative materials for temporary stands, is allowed without an Authorization, provided:

  o The items are not on the Prohibited or SCOMET List.

  o The exhibits are for use at exhibitions, fairs, or similar shows/displays.

- A bond or security is submitted to Customs or via an ATA Carnet.
- The duration of use is limited to six months, after which the items must be re-exported/re-imported.

### (b) Extensions:

- Requests for extensions beyond six months for re-export/re-import will be considered by Customs authorities based on the merits of the case.

### (c) Consumable Items:

- Items like paints, printed material, pamphlets, and literature related to exhibits:
  - Do not require re-export/re-import after the exhibition.
  - Extension of Bond Period for Exhibition Goods
  - If goods brought into India for exhibitions, fairs, or demonstrations are not re-exported or sold within the prescribed bond period, the Customs Authorities may grant an extension under the following conditions:

---

### Key Points for Extension of Bond Period

- Circumstances Beyond Control:
- The importer must demonstrate that the failure to re-export or sell the goods within the bond period occurred due to circumstances beyond their control.
- Examples:

- Delays caused by unforeseen events (natural disasters, logistical disruptions, etc.).

- Legal or regulatory hurdles.

- Cancellation or extension of the exhibition/event.

- Assessment on Merits:

- Customs Authorities will evaluate each case based on its individual merits.

- Factors considered:

- Reasonableness of the circumstances.

- Evidence provided by the importer.

- Documentation for Request:

- A formal request must be submitted to the Customs Authorities, including:

- Details of the goods and exhibition.

- Original bond documentation.

- Evidence supporting the claim for extension (e.g., letters from event organizers, shipping delays, etc.).

- A justification for why the extension is necessary.

- Extension Period:

- The length of the extension will be at the discretion of the Customs Authorities, depending on the justification and evidence provided.

- Conditions During Extension:

- The goods must continue to be accounted for and comply with Customs regulations.

- No contravention of the original terms of import (e.g., ATA Carnet rules or bond conditions).

- Customs Duty Implications:

- If the goods are eventually sold instead of being re-exported, applicable Customs duties and penalties (if any) must be paid as per existing regulations.

---

**Steps for Importer**

- Identify the Delay:

- As soon as it becomes clear that the goods cannot be re-exported or sold within the bond period, initiate the extension request process.

- Prepare Documentation:

- Collect all supporting documents to substantiate the claim for an extension.

- Submit Application:

- File a request with the relevant Customs office overseeing the bonded goods.

- Follow Up:

- Coordinate with Customs to ensure the request is processed in a timely manner.

- Personal car can also be imported temporarily under ATA Carnet issued by the export country and in

India FICCI will accept the ATA Carnet and undertaking whatever they dim fit.

- Any goods exported from India for exhibitions, it is advisable to obtain Ata carnet from FICCI, India. Generally agent assist for the same.

---

**2.61 Sale of Exhibits**

**(a) Sale of Restricted Items:**

- Restricted items listed in the ITC (HS), imported for international exhibitions or fairs, may be sold:
    - Without Authorization.
    - Within the bond period allowed for re-export.
    - On payment of applicable customs duties.
    - Ceiling Limit: ₹5 lakh (CIF) per exhibitor for such sales.

**(b) Sale of Freely Importable Items:**

- Sale of freely importable items exhibited at such events is allowed:
    - Within the bond period allowed for re-export.
    - On payment of applicable customs duties.

---

**Key Notes**

- Bond or Security Submission:

- - Necessary for temporary imports/exports unless processed under ATA Carnet.
- Customs Duties:
  - Applicable for all sales of restricted or freely importable items.
- Ceiling for Restricted Items:
  - ₹5 lakh (CIF) limit ensures regulated sales of restricted items at exhibitions.
- Extensions:
  - Extensions for re-export/re-import are discretionary and assessed individually.

**Let me know if you need more details or further clarifications!**

**Imports Facilitating Nepal and Government Use**

**(q) Goods Licensed by His Majesty's Government of Nepal:**

- Goods imported under an **import license** issued by the Nepalese government are exempt, provided:
  - The importer submits a **bond** with a scheduled bank as surety.
  - Duty and penalties are paid for any portion of goods that do not enter Nepal's territory.

**(r) Goods for Repair and Re-Export:**

- Goods of Indian manufacture imported by the **Central/State Government** for **repair and re-export** to:
  - Indian Embassies abroad, or
  - Other Central/State Government offices in foreign countries.

---

**Food and Aid-Related Imports**

**(s) Food Grains by the Food Corporation of India:**

- Food grains imported by the **Food Corporation of India** are exempt, provided:
  - A declaration is furnished at the time of clearance stating the import is **approved by the Central Government.**

**(t) Food and Edible Material as Free Gifts:**

- Articles of food and edible materials supplied as free gifts by United Nations-approved agencies are exempt as per Notification GSR 766 dated 21st June 1975.

---

**General Exemptions from Rules**

**(2) Goods Exempt from the Application of Rules:**

  - Goods **exported** by or under the authority of the **Central Government.**

- Goods other than foodstuffs that constitute the **stores or equipment** of any **outgoing vessel or conveyance**.

---

## Summary of Provisions

This section outlines comprehensive exemptions to promote trade facilitation, humanitarian aid, and international cooperation:

- **Specific exemptions** for temporary imports, government purposes, and international obligations.
- **Provisions for food and aid-related imports** for public welfare.
- Flexibility for **temporary vehicle imports** and re-export obligations under international conventions.

## Additional Provisions for Exemptions in Export and Transit of Goods

### (c) Bona Fide Personal Baggage

- Goods constituting **bona fide personal baggage** of any person (passenger or crew member) leaving India are exempt.
- **Exception**: Wildlife (dead, alive, parts, or products derived therefrom) is **not** considered part of personal baggage.

---

### (d) Goods Exported by Post or Air

- Goods exported via **post** or **air** are exempt if they comply with the conditions outlined in **postal notices** issued by the Postal Authorities.

---

### (e) Transhipped Goods

- Goods transhipped at an Indian port are exempt, provided they were **manifested for transshipment** during dispatch from a port outside India.

---

### (f) Goods Imported and Bonded for Re-Export

- Goods imported and bonded upon arrival in India for re-export to countries (excluding **Nepal** and **Bhutan**) are exempt.

---

### (g) Goods in Transit Through India

- Goods in transit through India (via **post** or redirected by post to a destination outside India, excluding **Nepal** and **Bhutan**) are exempt, provided they remain under the custody of the **postal authorities** while in India.

### (h) Goods Imported Without a Valid License and Exported by Customs Order

- Goods imported without a valid **import license** are exempt if exported under an order issued by the **Customs authority**.

---

### (i) Goods from Free Trade Zones/Export-Oriented Units

- Products approved for:
  - **Manufacture** and **export** from Free Trade Zones (FTZ), Export Processing Zones (EPZ), or 100% Export-Oriented Units (EOUs).
  - Exclusions:
    - Textile items covered by bilateral agreements.
    - Exports to **Rupee payment countries** under the Annual Trade Protocol.
    - Exports against payment in Indian Rupees to former Rupee payment countries.
- Conditions:
  - Units must comply with the terms outlined in their **Letter of Approval** or **Letter of Intent**.

---

### (j) Export of Blood Group Oh (Bombay Phenotype)

- Export of Blood Group Oh (Bombay Phenotype) for:
  - Scientific research.

- o Emergency medical treatment on humanitarian grounds.
- Authorized by the **Director, National Blood Group Reference Laboratory, Bombay**, with a certificate issued for each case.

---

### (k) Export of Samples of Petroleum and Related Products

- Samples of:
  - o Lubricating oil additives, lube oil, crude oil, and other petroleum products.
  - o Raw materials used in manufacturing lube additives.
- Exported by:
  - o Lubrizol India Limited, Hindustan Petroleum Corporation Limited, and Bharat Petroleum Corporation Limited.
- Purpose:
  - o For evaluation and testing at Lubrizol's Laboratories in the United States and United Kingdom.

---

### Final Authorization

This comprehensive exemption order is issued under the authority of Dr. P.L. Sanjeev Reddy, Director General of Foreign Trade and Ex-Officio Additional Secretary.

[File No. 21/11/92-LS]

**Tips for Packing and Shipping Personal Effects**

**1. Accompanied Baggage**

- Packing Guidelines:
    - Pack items in suitcases or cardboard boxes.
    - Ensure that each package's cubic measurement does not exceed 60 inches.
- Excess Baggage:
    - Airlines charge extra for excess baggage.
    - **Save Money**:
        - Check airline-specific discounts for online purchase of additional baggage allowances.
        - For instance, **Emirates** offers:
        - Discounts for pre-purchasing extra baggage online or at retail/contact centers.
        - Purchase via the **Manage Your Booking** section using your ticket reference number, up to **four hours before departure**.

---

**2. Unaccompanied Baggage**

- Booking Period:
    - Goods can be shipped as cargo within **one year of departure** by **air** or **sea**.
- Contact Freight Forwarders:

- Use a reliable freight forwarder for **door-to-door** handling.
- Ensure the agent has a **valid customs license** to avoid inconvenience.

- Documents Required:
  - Self-attested **passport copy**.
  - **Visa page/green card**.
  - **Air tickets** and boarding pass (if available).
  - **PAN card** (for Indian citizens).
  - **Packing list**.
  - **Authority letter**.
  - **Appointment letter** (if applicable for job-related moves).
  - **Origin and destination address** with contact numbers.
  - **Email ID**.

- Insurance:
  - Always insure your goods for safe transit.

---

## 3. Shipping Costs.

- Courier Shipments (< 50 kg):
  - It's cost-effective to use courier services.

- Courier Costs range from ₹1,000 to ₹1,500 per kg, depending on the destination.

- Weight Calculation:
  - Air shipments are charged based on gross weight or volume weight (whichever is higher).
  - Volume weight calculation for:
  - Air Cargo: formula how to calculate volume weight
    Volume Weight Length (cm) × Widths (cm) × Hight (cm) divide 6000 = volume weight
  - Example: 56x56x24inches divide 6000 kg = 12.5 kg
    - **Courier:** formula how to calculate volume weight
      Volume Weight L (cm) × W (cm) × H (cm) divide 5000 = volume weight
    - Example: For dimensions 56x56x24 cm, Volume weight via courier: 56×56×24inches divide 5000=15 kg

---

## 4. Sea Freight

- Types of Shipments:
  - Less Container Load (LCL):
    - Suitable for smaller volumes.
    - Charged based on volume.

- Full Container Load (FCL): type and size of containers
    - 1x20ft approximately 1000 cubic ft or 28.5 cubic meter
    - 1x40ft approximately 2000 cubic ft or 57 cubic meter
    - 1x40ft HQ 2200 cubic ft or 63 cubic meter
- Volume Calculation for LCL:
    - Volume L x width x Hight divide 1728 = cubic ft divide 35 - cubic meter
    - example
    - 60x50x48 inches divide 1728 = 83 cubic feet divide 35 = 2.38 cbm

---

**Additional Tips**

- Verify Agents:
    - Ensure freight forwarders or agents are authorized and licensed to avoid issues.
- Plan Early:
    - Compare costs for air, courier, and sea shipping to select the most cost-effective option.
- Label Clearly:

- o Properly label packages with both **origin** and **destination addresses**.
- Track Shipments:
  - o Use tracking services provided by the freight or courier company.

**Packing, Shipping, and Airway Bill (AWB) Guidelines for Personal Effects**

---

### 1. Packing Guidelines

- Cartons:
  - o Use **7-ply cartons**, crafted cardboard, bubble wrap, foam, and shrink-wrapping films.
  - o Fragile items should be crated for extra protection.
- Safety:
  - o For **Less Container Load (LCL)** shipments, goods should be packed in **wooden lift vans** for better safety and security.

---

### 2. Shipping Volume Calculation

- Volume in Cubic Meters (CBM):
  - o Formula: L x W x H= inches divide 1728 = cubic feet divide 35 = cubic metre
  - o Example:
    - Dimensions: 120 × 100 × 70 inches

- how to calculate cubic ft and cubic meter 120×100×70 divide 1728=486 cubic feet divide 35 = 13.88 cbm

---

## 3. Container Specifications

- Full Container Load (FCL) Sizes:
  - 20 ft container: Capacity 900 cubic feet (cft).
  - 40 ft container: Capacity 1900 cft.
  - 40 ft HQ container: Capacity 2200 cft.

---

## 4. Survey for Volume Assessment

- Packers generally request:
  - **Video survey** or **physical survey** to assess the volume of goods.
  - Based on the survey, they quote for:
    - Door-to-door or door-to-port services.
    - Container options: LCL, 20 ft FCL, 40 ft FCL, or 40 ft HQ FCL.
    - Specimen of documents for export shipments

Date:

**S P E C I M E N S**

To,

The Deputy Commissioner of Customs

I.G.I. Airport

New Delhi.

# Sub : Authority Letter

Dear Sir,

We hereby authorize M/s Ashoka International, New Delhi, CHA No. 9/87 valid upto 14/09/2025 to export my to on my behalf risk and responsibility.

Kindly allow M/s Ashoka International, New Delhi to submit the documents accordingly.

Thanking you,

✗

**(Signature of Passenger)**

SPECIMENS

To,

The Deputy Commissioner of Customs
Export Shed, IGI Airport
New Delhi.

Dear Sir,

I hereby authorize M/s Ashoka International, New Delhi, CHA No. 9/87 valid upto 14/09/2025 to export my used Household Goods and Personal Effects to _____ on my behalf, risk and responsibility.

Further, I am under orders of official transfer & do hereby declare that the food stuff in my consignment is meant to my personal consumption not for any sale.

Kindly allow M/s. Ashoka International, New Delhi to submit the documents accordingly.

Thanking you,

✗

(Signature of Passenger)

S P E C I M E N S

## TO WHOM SO IT MAY CONCERN

We hereby certify that the contents of the consignments are not dangerous goods and are not dangerous of carrying by air according to the current 66$^{th}$ Edition for IATA Dangerous Goods regulations and all applicable carrier and Government regulations.

We acknowledge that we may be liable for Dangerous resulting from any misstatement or omission and we further agree that any air carrier involved in the shipment of the consignment may rely upon this certificate.

1. NO OF PKGS :
2. PRODCUT NAME :
3. GROSS WEIGHT :
4. NET WEIGHT :
5. DESTINATION :
6. CONSIGNEE ADDRESS :
7. AWB NO. :
8. NOTIFY ADDRESS : SAME AS ABOVE

**x (SIGNATURE OF PASSENGER)**

S P E C I M E N S

## TO WHOM SO IT MAY CONCERN

We hereby certify that the contents of the consignments are not dangerous goods and are not dangerous of carrying by air according to the current 66$^{th}$ Edition for IATA Dangerous Goods regulations and all applicable carrier and Government regulations.

We acknowledge that we may be liable for Dangerous resulting from any misstatement or omission and we further agree that any air carrier involved in the shipment of the consignment may rely upon this certificate.

1. NO OF PKGS :
2. PRODCUT NAME :
3. GROSS WEIGHT :
4. NET WEIGHT :
5. DESTINATION :
6. CONSIGNEE ADDRESS :
7. AWB NO. :
8. NOTIFY ADDRESS : SAME AS ABOVE

**"THIS CARGO HAS NOT ORIGINATED IN EITHER YEMEN, EGYPT, SYRIA & SOMALIA"**


**x (SIGNATURE OF PASSENGER)**

Date: _____

S P E C I ME N S

___NAME OF THE
SHIPPINGLINE_____

_____

_____

_____

_____

_____

Kind Attention : Import Department

Subject: Container No._____ and B/L No. _____ containing Personal Household Effects

Dear Sir,

I hereby authorize M/s Ashoka International, New Delhi to collect the Delivery Order on my behalf in respect of my above consignment.

Thanking You,

Yours truly,

(                                   )

Name:

S P E C I M E N S

The Deputy Collector of Customs,

(Import Shed)

ICD, Tughlakabad,

New Delhi

                                            Dated:

Subject: Custom clearance -used personal and household effects under

Container No. _____

Dear Sir,

    I, _____ holder of Diplomatic/Official Passport No. _____, have recently returned on posting to Headquarter, i.e. Ministry of External Affairs, New Delhi on transfer from _____. My household and personal effects have already been reached at ICD, Tkd under above mentioned container.

Due to some official engagements, I am unable to be personally present at ICD Depot for attending to various procedures/formalities for clearance of my above consignment.

I hereby authorize Mr._____of Ashoka International, New Delhi to handle the custom formalities and take delivery of my goods on my behalf.

Thanking you in anticipation.

Yours faithfully,


(                    )

S P E C I M E N S

Date:

The Deputy Commissioner of Customs

ICD/CFS/IGI Airport

New Delhi

Subject: Container No._____ and B/L No._____

Containing personal household effects

Dear Sir,

      I hereby authorize M/s Ashoka International, New Delhi to attend custom clearance and take delivery of my Household goods/Car on my behalf, risk and responsibility.

      Please allow them to submit papers on my behalf.

Thanking you,

Yours truly,

(                )

Name:

Address & Tel No.

SPECIMENS

Date: _____

_____
_____
_____
_____
_____
_____

Kind Attention: Import Department

Subject: No Objection Certificate for refund of Security Deposit vide Container No._____ and B/L No. _____ containing Personal Household Effects

Dear Sir,

An Amount of Rs. _____is paid by M/s Ashoka International as security deposit for custom clearance of above container on my behalf.

You are requested to please release/refund the security amount to them and issue cheque in the name of M/s Ashoka International

Thanking You,

Yours truly,

(                              )

Name:

SPECIMENS

The Deputy Commissioner of Customs,

Inland Container Depot, Tughlakabad

New Delhi

Dated : _____/2025

Regarding: Condonation delay in Shipment -BL NO. _____

Dear Sir,

      I, _____holder of Diplomatic/official passport No _____ have returned on posting from_____ to New Delhi after completion of my official tenure. My unaccompanied baggage has arrived ICD, New Delhi under above mentioned bill of lading

I landed India on _____ and handed over my baggage for shipment to Indian Embassy/HCI agent before my departure to dispatch of goods to India. The shipment could not be affected before _____ due to non-availability of vessel/containers and pandemic.

In view of above, kindly condone the delay in shipment which has caused due to above stated reason. The delay is beyond my control and transfer is in public interest.

Thanking you for your anticipation.

Yours sincerely,

(              )

**Signature required**

## Unaccompanied Baggage Declaration Form

| | | | |
|---|---|---|---|
| Name of Passenger | | Date of Departure from India | |
| Address | | Date of arrival in India | |
| | | Baggage Type [TR/MTR/NTR]* | |
| City | | Whether you have availed TR in the past | |
| State | | | |
| PIN | | Date of availment of TR | |
| Phone | | | |
| Sex (M/F) | | IGM No. | |
| Nationality | | Date of IGM | |
| Passport No. | | MAWB No. | |
| Passport is valid upto | | Date of MAWB | |
| | | HAWB No. | |
| Baggage consigned from the country | | Date of HAWB | |
| | | No. of packages | |
| Port of loading | | Gross weight in Kg | |
| Any short visits (Yes/No) during the preceding two years (for TR/MTR only) | | | |
| If yes above, details of short visits | | | |
| | | | |

| Details of the Items imported | | | | | |
|---|---|---|---|---|---|
| S. No. | Item Description | Brand | Quantity | Unit Price | Total Value |
|  |  |  |  |  |  |

DECLARATION

I hereby declare that the particulars given above are true

[Signature of Passenger]

TR – Transfer of Residence

MTR – Mini Transfer of Residence

NTR – Other than TR & MTR

S P E C I ME N S , documentations

Dear Sir,,

We have been awarded the Job of packing and forwarding your shipment to

Lilongwe

We are enclosing the following specimens required for the export of your personal

household effects from New Delhi to Lilongwe.

Two letters addressed to Dy. Commissioner Customs ICD (Tughlakabad) (to be

typed on office letterhead-02 Original copies)

DCP Traffic Police Letter

We need the following documents from your side.

1. Passport photocopy (self-attested) .

2. Visa Copy (Self attested)

3. Transfer Order Copy

4. Pan card copy (self-attested)

5. Flight Ticket copy with Ticket number

6. Insurance Break-up of your household goods – as per your entitlement

We hope you will find the above documents are in order.

Regards,

Divya

S P E C I M E N S , letters for permission of factory/House stuffing of container

GOVT OF INDIA

MINISTRY OF EXTERNAL AFFAIRS

NEW DELHI

The Deputy Commissioner of Customs,

ICD (Tuglakabad)/CFS Patparganj

New Delhi.

Sub: Permission for House / ICD Stuffing of Personal Effects

Dear Sir,

This is to inform that I, _____ proceeding on transfer to Embassy of

India, Lilongwe. I am holder of passport No. _____ issued on

_____ valid up to _____. I am sending my used household goods

and personal effects from New Delhi to Lilongwe.

I shall be grateful if you could kindly give necessary permission to stuff my personal effects at my residence at

_____

__ I undertake to

return the container, after stuffing within seven days, at the above-mentioned address for

onward shipment to Lilongwe.

I have no objection if however, the container is opened at ICD for customs examination and

hereby authorize Ashoka International to handle the export of this shipment on my behalf.

I certify that shipment does not contain any thing that is not permitted / banned for export from

India especially that it does not contain pornographic material, silverware, Ivory, skin of animals,

antiques, drugs etc. and no gift parcel are carried by me. The packing has been personally

supervised by me.

Please allow the shipment be sent to Lilongwe at the earliest.

Thanking you,

Yours faithfully

( )

## SPECIMENS

GOVT OF INDIA

MINISTRY OF EXTERNAL AFFAIRS

NEW DELHI

The Deputy Commissioner of Customs,

ICD (Tuglakabad)/CFS Patparganj

New Delhi.

Sub: Shipment of Household goods and Personal Effects to Ulaanbatar

Dear Sir,

This is to inform that I, _____ proceeding on transfer to

Embassy of India, Ulaanbatar. I am holder of passport No. _____ issued on

_____ valid upto _____. I am sending my used household goods

and personal effects from New Delhi to Ulaanbaatar

I have no objection if however, the container is opened at ICD for customs examination

and hereby authorize Ashoka International to handle the export of this shipment on my behalf.

I certify that shipment does not contain any thing that is not permitted / banned for export from

India especially that it does not contain pornographic material, silverware, Ivory, skin of animals,

antiques, drugs etc. and no gift parcel are carried by me. The packing has been personally

supervised by me.

Please allow the shipment be sent to Ulaanbatar at earliest.

Thanking you,

Yours faithfully

SPECIMENS

The D.C.P Traffic Police,

New Delhi

Dear Sir,

We will be grateful if you could allow the Truck No _____ to come from ICD / CFS to

_____ for loading of Household goods for onward shipment to Lilongwe.

It will be appreciated if permission is given to bring the container at _____ and back to ICD

/CFS during no-entry period from 8.00 a.m. to 10.00 p.m on

_____.

We hereby authorize M/s Ashoka International to collect the permission on our behalf.

Thanking you,

Yours faithfully,

# SPECIMENS

## ON LETTERHEAD

The Deputy Commissioner of Customs,

ICD (Tuglakabad)/CFS Patparganj

New Delhi.

Sub: Permission for House / ICD Stuffing of Personal Effects

Dear Sir,

This is to inform that I, _____ proceeding on Bucharest after finishing

my tenure from_____. I am holder of passport No. _____ issued on

_____ valid upto _____. I am sending my used household goods

and personal effects from New Delhi to Bucharest.

I shall be grateful if you could kindly give necessary permission to stuff my personal effects at

my residence at _____
__ I undertake to

return the container, after stuffing within seven days, at the above-mentioned address for onward shipment to Bucharest.

The Container is sealed with Embassy seal and please do not open for custom examination

as he enjoys Diplomatic Privileges in India. We hereby authorize Ashoka International to

handle the export of this shipment on my behalf.

I certify that shipment does not contain any thing that is not permitted / banned for export from

India especially that it does not contain pornographic material, silverware, Ivory, skin of animals,

antiques, drugs etc. and no gift parcel are carried by me. The packing has been personally

supervised by me.

Please allow the shipment be sent to Bucharest at the earliest.

Thanking you,

Yours faithfully

( )

S P E C I M E N S

ON LETTERHEAD

The Deputy Commissioner of Customs,

ICD (Tuglakabad)/CFS Patparganj

New Delhi.

Sub: Shipment of Household goods and Personal Effects to Bucharest

Dear Sir,

This is to inform that I, _____ proceeding on Bucharest after

finishing my tenure from_____. I am holder of passport No. _____

issued on _____ valid up to _____. I am sending my used

household goods and personal effects from New Delhi to Bucharest.

The Container is sealed with Embassy seal and please do not open for custom examination

as he enjoys Diplomatic Privileges in India. We hereby authorize Ashoka International to

handle the export of this shipment on my behalf.

I certify that shipment does not contain any thing that is not permitted / banned for export from

India especially that it does not contain pornographic material, silverware, Ivory, skin of animals,

antiques, drugs etc. and no gift parcel are carried by me. The packing has been personally

supervised by me.

Please allow the shipment be sent to Bucharest at earliest.

Thanking you,

Yours faithfully


(                    )

S P E C I M E N S

The D.C.P Traffic Police,

New Delhi

Dear Sir,

We will be grateful if you could allow the Truck No

_____
_____to come from ICD / CFS to

_____
_____fo
r loading of Household

goods for onward shipment to Bucharest.

It will be appreciated if permission is given to bring the container at

_____
_____ and back to ICD /CFS during no-entry

period from 8.00 a.m. to 10.00 p.m on _____.

We hereby authorize M/s Ashoka International to collect the permission on our behalf.

Thanking you,

Yours faithfully,

## 5. Specimen for Airway Bill (AWB) Instructions

| Field | Details |
|---|---|
| Exporter | Client Name (as per Passport) |
| | C/O Ministry of External Affairs |
| | Jawaharlal Nehru Bhawan, New Delhi, India |
| Consignee | Client Name (as per Passport) |
| | Destination Address |
| | Tel: |
| | Email ID: |
| Notify Party | Same as Consignee |
| Port of Loading | New Delhi (or any other city) |
| Port of Destination | Delivery Airport |
| Number of Packets | |
| Gross Weight | ___ KGS |
| Volume Weight | ___ KGS |
| Dimensions (in CMS) | |
| Commodity | Household Goods & Personal Effects |
| Passport No. | |
| Flight | Example: DEL to LHR – 19-19-2032 – AI 111 |
| Ticket No. | XXXXXXXXXX |

## 6. Additional Tips

- Plan Well:
  - Ensure all documents are ready in advance.
  - Double-check measurements for accurate volume and weight calculations.
- Insurance:
  - Insure goods to avoid losses during transit.
- Licensed Agents:
  - Always engage authorized agents with valid customs licenses for handling shipments.
- Mode of Shipment:
  - **Air Freight**: Faster but costlier. Calculate volume weight carefully.
  - **Sea Freight**: Ideal for bulk shipments; use LCL or FCL based on volume.

---

This guide provides a complete overview of the process, from packing to filling an AWB for export shipments.

## Specimen for Bill of Lading (BL) / Sea Waybill (SWB) Instructions

| Field | Details |
|---|---|
| Exporter | Client Name (as per Passport) |
| | C/O Ministry of External Affairs |
| | Jawaharlal Nehru Bhawan, New Delhi, India |
| Consignee | Client Name (as per Passport) |
| | Destination Address |
| | Tel: |
| | Email ID: |
| Notify Party | Same as Consignee |
| Port of Loading | New Delhi (or any other applicable city) |
| Port of Destination | Delivery Port (Specify the final delivery airport or sea port) |
| Number of Packets | |
| Gross Weight | ___ KGS |
| Volume Weight | ___ KGS |
| Dimensions (in CMS) | |
| Commodity | Household Goods & Personal Effects |
| Passport No. | |
| Flight | DEL to LHR – 19-19-2032 – AI 111 |
| Ticket No. | XXXXXXXXXX |

**Instructions for Filling the BL/SWB**

- Exporter Details:
  - Include the full **name, address**, and any relevant identifiers (e.g., passport number).
- Consignee Details:
  - Ensure the **name, address, telephone number**, and **email ID** are accurate for proper communication.
- Notify Party:
  - Typically, the same as the consignee unless otherwise specified.
- Ports:
  - Clearly mention the **Port of Loading** (origin) and **Port of Destination** (delivery point).
- Weights and Dimensions:
  - Accurately record the **gross weight, volume weight**, and **dimensions** of the shipment for freight calculation.
- Commodity Description:
  - Specify the contents of the shipment, such as "Household Goods & Personal Effects."
- Passport Details:
  - Provide the **passport number** of the shipper for documentation.
- Flight Details:

o  For air cargo, specify the **flight number** and **date**.

---

**Additional Notes:**

- Always verify all details before submitting to ensure smooth customs clearance.
- Cross-check weights and dimensions to avoid discrepancies in freight charges.
- Maintain copies of all documents for records and potential queries.

**Import Process for Baggage to India: AWB and Bill of Lading (SWB) Instructions**

1. Airway Bill (AWB) Instructions for Import to India

For importing baggage to India via air, you can request your packers/relocation company to prepare the AWB as follows:

| Field | Details |
|---|---|
| Shipper | Name of client (as per passport) |
| | Full address at the origin |
| Consignee | Name of client (as per passport) |
| | Address in India & Contact Number |
| Notify | Ashoka International |
| | 21, DDA Market, Munirka Vihar, New Delhi |
| APOE | New Delhi |

- **Approval**: Share the draft AWB with **Ashoka International** for approval before printing the final copy.

---

## 2. Bill of Lading (SWB) Instructions for Import to India

When importing baggage to India via sea, ask your origin agent to prepare the Bill of Lading or Sea Waybill as per the format below:

| Field | Details |
| --- | --- |
| **Shipper** | Name of client (as per passport) |
| | Full address at the origin |
| | Contact number |
| **Consignee** | Name of client (as per passport) |
| | Address in India (as per passport) |
| | Contact number |
| | IEC: 0100000045 |
| **Notify** | Ashoka International |
| | 21, DDA Market, 1st Floor, Munirka Vihar, Nelson Mandela Marg, New Delhi |
| | Tel: 26177214 |
| | Email: ashokaint@gmail.com |

| Field | Details |
|---|---|
| | GST No.: 07AAOPK0482E1ZR |
| Port of Discharge | Mundra / Nhava Sheva |
| Final Place of Delivery | ICD, New Delhi |

---

**Key Notes**

- Freight & IHC:
    - Freight and Inland Haulage Charges (IHC) must be prepaid up to ICD, New Delhi.
- Draft B/L Approval:
    - Share the draft Bill of Lading with **Ashoka International** for approval before finalizing.
    - A **Master Bill of Lading (MB/L)** is required, and it must be either **Sea Waybill (SWB)** or **Telex Release**.
    - **Original B/L is not required**.
- Supporting Documents:
    - Ensure the following documents are ready:
        - Copy of the **passport**.
        - **Packing inventory list** for the baggage.

- Free Detention Period:
  - Request a **14-day detention-free period** from the shipping line at the final destination (ICD, New Delhi) to avoid extra charges.

---

**Contact Information**

For clarification, assistance, or further guidance, reach out to **Ashoka International**:

- Email:
  - ashok@ashokaint.com
  - moving@ashokaint.com
- Phone:
  - +91 26177214

Ashoka International has been in the relocation trade since **1977** and offers expert advice and current updates on customs and import regulations.

Let me know if you need any further guidance!

**Import Process for Baggage to India: AWB and Bill of Lading (SWB) Instructions**

**1. Airway Bill (AWB) Instructions for Import to India**

For importing baggage to India via air, you can request your packers/relocation company to prepare the AWB as follows:

| Field | Details |
|---|---|
| **Shipper** | Name of client (as per passport) |
| | Full address at the origin |
| **Consignee** | Name of client (as per passport) |
| | Address in India & Contact Number |
| **Notify** | Ashoka International |
| | 21, DDA Market, Munirka Vihar, New Delhi |
| **APOE** | New Delhi |

- **Approval**: Share the draft AWB with **Ashoka International** for approval before printing the final copy.

---

## 2. Bill of Lading (SWB) Instructions for Import to India

When importing baggage to India via sea, ask your origin agent to prepare the Bill of Lading or Sea Waybill as per the format below:

| Field | Details |
|---|---|
| **Shipper** | Name of client (as per passport) |
| | Full address at the origin |
| | Contact number |
| **Consignee** | Name of client (as per passport) |

| Field | Details |
|---|---|
| | Address in India (as per passport) |
| | Contact number |
| | IEC: 0100000045 |
| Notify | Ashoka International |
| | 21, DDA Market, 1st Floor, Munirka Vihar, Nelson Mandela Marg, New Delhi |
| | Tel: 26177214 |
| | Email: ashokaint@gmail.com |
| | GST No.: 07AAOPK0482E1ZR |
| Port of Discharge | Mundra / Nhava Sheva |
| Final Place of Delivery | ICD, New Delhi |

**Key Notes**

- Freight & IHC:
  - Freight and Inland Haulage Charges (IHC) must be prepaid up to ICD, New Delhi.
- Draft B/L Approval:
  - Share the draft Bill of Lading with **Ashoka International** for approval before finalizing.

- A Master Bill of Lading (MB/L) is required, and it must be either Sea Waybill (SWB) or Telex Release.
- Original B/L is not required.

- Supporting Documents:
  - Ensure the following documents are ready:
    - Copy of the **passport**.
    - **Packing inventory list** for the baggage.

- Free Detention Period:
  - Request a **14-day detention-free period** from the shipping line at the final destination (ICD, New Delhi) to avoid extra charges.

---

**Contact Information**

For clarification, assistance, or further guidance, reach out to **Ashoka International**:

- Email:
  - ashok@ashokaint.com
  - moving@ashokaint.com
- Phone:
  - +91 26177214

Ashoka International has been in the relocation trade since **1977** and offers expert advice and current updates on customs and import regulations.

Let me know if you need any further guidance!

www.ingramcontent.com/pod-product-compliance
Lightning Source LLC
LaVergne TN
LVHW041612070526
838199LV00052B/3110